Contents

Reptiles in the animal kingdom

Reptiles belong to the animal kingdom, a group that includes all animals. Here are some of the main groups in the animal kingdom.

reptiles

cold-blooded animals with backbones; dry scales cover a reptile's body

cold-blooded

reptiles have a body temperature that is the same as the temperature of their surroundings; reptiles bask, or lie in the sunshine to warm up

mammals

warm-blooded animals that have backbones and hair or fur instead of scales; female mammals feed milk to their young

insects

small animals with hard outer shells, six legs, three body sections and two antennae; most insects have wings

birds

warm-blooded animals that have feathers and wings and can lay eggs

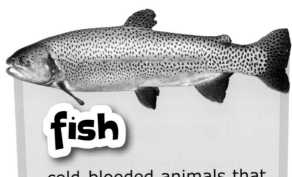

fish

cold-blooded animals that live in water and have scales, fins and gills

amphibians

cold-blooded animals with backbones and wet skin

Amphibians aren't reptiles

larva

most amphibians are born as larvae that look very different from adults; baby reptiles look like small adults

egg

amphibians have smooth, wet skin while reptiles have dry, scaly skin; amphibians can also breathe through their skin

skin

amphibian eggs are soft; reptiles lay hard or leathery eggs

Meet the reptiles

From creeping crocodiles to slithering snakes, reptiles live almost everywhere on Earth. There are more than 8,000 kinds of reptiles, which scientists have divided into groups. Here are some of the most common groups.

alligators and crocodiles

large reptiles that have strong jaws and sharp teeth used to kill other animals; alligators and crocodiles spend much of their time in the water

crocodile

Alligator or crocodile?

jaw

alligators have U-shaped jaws while crocodiles have V-shaped jaws; an alligator's bottom teeth are not visible when its jaws are closed, but a crocodile's are

turtles and tortoises

reptiles that can pull their heads, legs and tails into their hard shells for protection; turtles live in water and on land, but tortoises live only on land

tuataras

lizardlike reptiles that live only in New Zealand; they sleep during the day and hunt at night

geckos

small, harmless lizards often found in houses in warm countries; geckos make squeaking and barking sounds

chameleons

lizards that can change their skin colour

iguanas

lizards with four legs and long tails; green iguanas can grow to be more than 1.5 metres (5 feet) long

colubrids

boomslang

more than half of all snakes belong to the colubrid family; both deadly boomslangs and harmless garter snakes are colubrids

cobras

large, venomous snakes; some cobras spread their neck skin to look like a hood

vipers

family of venomous snakes, such as rattlesnakes

pythons

large, powerful snakes that wrap themselves around prey and suffocate it; female pythons lay eggs

boas

tropical snakes that kill their prey by wrapping around it and squeezing; female boas give birth to live young

beaded lizards

large, slow-moving lizards found in Mexico, Guatemala and the southwestern United States; a beaded lizard called the Gila monster is the only venomous lizard in the United States

skinks

the largest lizard family; skinks are slow-moving and have small legs

worm lizards

a kind of lizard that looks like a snake; these reptiles dig tunnels and live underground

monitor lizards

lizards with long necks, short bodies and strong tails

From egg to adult

life cycle

the series of changes that take place in a living thing, from birth to death; the life cycle for most reptiles begins with an egg

life span

the number of years a certain animal usually lives; sand lizards can live for 12 years

egg tooth

a sharp bump on top of a lizard's or snake's snout, used to cut itself out of an egg

hatchling

a young reptile that has just come out of its egg

nest to build a nest, the female sand lizard digs a hole in sandy soil

guard

to watch over and keep safe; unlike most reptiles, crocodiles guard their young

egg layers most reptiles lay eggs

clutch a group of eggs; the female sand lizard lays four to 14 eggs in the nest, covers them and leaves

hatch

to break out of an egg; after about two months, the young sand lizards hatch; they live on their own after hatching

live birth

some snakes and lizards give live birth instead of laying eggs

What reptiles look like

Scaly skin. Long tails. Sharp teeth. Reptiles might look scary, but their body parts help them find food and stay safe.

teeth
most reptiles have teeth; alligator and crocodile teeth are lost and replaced thousands of times

beak
the hard, pointed part of an animal's mouth; turtles have no teeth – they use their pointy beaks to cut food

shell
a hard, outer covering that keeps turtles safe

webbed feet
feet with wide flaps of skin between the toes; a turtle's webbed feet help it swim; tortoises live on land and do not have webbed feet

fang

a long, hollow tooth

forked tongue

the moveable muscle in the mouths of snakes, beaded lizards and monitor lizards; the forked tongue is used to collect smells

snout

the long front part of a reptile's face, including its nose, mouth and jaws

dewlap

loose skin that hangs under the chin or neck of some reptiles

claw

a hard curved nail on the foot of some reptiles used for climbing, fighting and digging

scale

one of the small, hard plates that covers a reptile's body

sticky tongue

chameleons shoot out their long, sticky tongues to catch insects

Skin and scales

A reptile's dry, scaly skin might look strange, but for reptiles, dry skin is good! It helps keep water inside their bodies. Take a closer look at the skin and scales of reptiles.

keeled scales

scales that have ridges running down their centres

clear scales

a snake doesn't have eyelids that move; instead, clear scales cover a snake's eyes

keratin

hard material that makes up a reptile's scales; your fingernails are also made of keratin

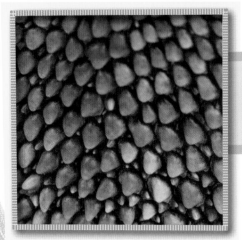

granular scales

small, bumpy scales that don't overlap

moult

to shed the outer layer of skin so new skin can grow; some lizards eat the dead skin they shed because nutrients in the skin help them grow

smooth scales

scales that have a regular or even surface, without roughness or bumps

armour

bones, scales or skin that some animals have on their bodies for protection; crocodiles have bony plates in their skin

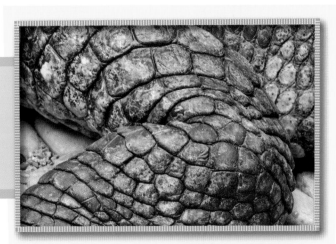

A turtle's shell

Can you imagine carrying your home on your back?
A turtle's shell protects its head, limbs and body.
All turtles have shells, but they don't all look the same.

carapace
the top part of a turtle's shell

scute
one of the large, hard scales that covers a turtle's shell

plastron
bottom part of a turtle's shell

skeleton
a turtle's shell is part of its skeleton; 50 to 60 bones make up a turtle's shell

exhale

turtles push the air out of their lungs to make room for their heads and legs inside their shells

ring

as turtles grow, their scutes make rings on their shells; scientists count the rings to tell how old a turtle is

straight-neck turtles

to stay safe, some turtles can pull their heads and legs completely into their shells

side-neck turtles

not all turtles can pull their heads and legs into their shells; a side-neck turtle turns its head sideways and tucks it against its shell

soft shell

some turtle shells are covered with leathery skin instead of scutes

What's for dinner?

Most reptiles eat other animals, but some snack on plants. Take a look at what's on a reptile's menu.

prey

animal hunted by another animal for food; many reptiles hunt insects, mammals, birds or fish

squeeze

boas and pythons squeeze prey to death before eating it; some boas and pythons can live for a year on a single meal

carnivore

animal that eats only meat; most reptiles are carnivores; all crocodiles and snakes eat only meat

predator

an animal that hunts other animals for food; most reptiles are predators

swallow

snakes don't chew their food; they swallow it whole

omnivore

animal that eats both plants and animals; sea turtles eat plants, fish and crabs

herbivore

animal that eats only plants; some lizards and turtles are herbivores

algae

small plants without roots or stems that grow in water; marine iguanas are the only lizards that eat algae

Reptiles on the move

They run! They swim! They fly through the air!
Watch out for reptiles on the move.

flipper

one of the broad, flat limbs of a sea creature; flippers push sea turtles through the ocean

migrate

move from one place to another when seasons change in order to find food or to lay eggs; female sea turtles return to the beaches where they were born to lay their eggs

grip

geckos have sticky toes that grip almost any surface; they can even hang upside down

slither

snakes move muscles in their bodies to slide along the ground

dive

marine iguanas swish their tails from side to side to dive for algae

glide

flying dragons glide between rainforest trees by spreading out folds of skin on the sides of their bodies; they can glide around 60 metres (200 feet) in a single leap

sprint

a short, fast run; basilisks run on their back legs; folds of skin along the sides of their toes help them dart across water

Slow and Fast

Galàpagos tortoise

tortoises are one of the slowest reptiles; the average person walks 17 times faster than the Galàpagos tortoise

the spiny-tailed iguana is the fastest reptile on land; it runs at speeds of 35 kilometres (22 miles) per hour

spiny-tailed iguana

Reptile senses

Do you spot a resting reptile? Reptiles keep busy even when they're not moving. They use their senses to escape danger and find their next meal.

slit pupil

the pupil is the dark centre of a reptile's eye that lets in light; reptiles that are active at night have slit pupils

taste bud

one of the small organs on the top of the tongue that tells animals and people what things taste like; lizards and crocodiles have taste buds, but snakes do not

round pupil

reptiles that are active during the day, such as iguanas, have round pupils

eye movement

chameleons can move each eye on its own; they can look at two different objects at the same time

third eye

lizards and tuataras have a "third eye" on the tops of their heads that is covered with scales; although the third eye cannot see, it may help lizards sense what time of day it is

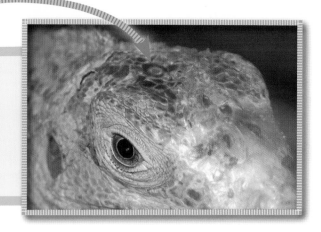

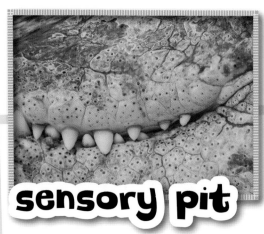

sensory pit

alligators and crocodiles have small, black speckles on their jaws called sensory pits; these pits help them feel movement in the water made by their prey

Jacobson's organ

an organ on the roof of the mouth of snakes and lizards; the tongue picks up scents and carries them to the Jacobson's organ

heat pit

pythons, boas and pit vipers use pits on their faces to feel the heat from their prey; the heat tells snakes when prey is near

python

vibration

fast movement back and forth; snakes don't "hear" with ears – they feel vibrations that move through the ground

Home sweet home

From deserts to oceans, reptiles live in almost every habitat on Earth. Some hang out in the treetops. Others burrow underground. Reptiles make their homes on every continent except Antarctica.

rainforest

a thick area of trees where rain falls almost every day; large numbers of snakes and lizards live in rainforests

ocean

a large body of salt water; the ocean is home to sea turtles, sea snakes and marine iguanas

adaptation

change a living thing goes through over time to better fit in with its environment; snakes that live in trees are long and thin in order to help them to climb

desert

dry area that gets little rain; many deserts are hot and sandy; lizards are the most common type of reptile found in deserts

burrow

a tunnel or hole in the ground made or used by an animal; desert reptiles enter their burrows to escape the heat

hibernate

spend the winter in a deep sleep; reptiles that live in colder places hibernate

freshwater

water that does not contain salt; turtles, crocodiles and snakes live in rivers, streams, ponds and lakes

nocturnal

active at night; desert and rainforest geckos escape the heat by resting during the day

Sneaky survivors

Lizards that spit blood. Snakes that play dead. Reptiles have found lots of sneaky ways to survive. They hide from enemies but also use defences to stay safe.

blood

horned lizards squirt blood from their eyes to scare away predators

startle

surprise or frighten; blue-tongued skinks stick out their brightly coloured tongues and hiss to scare away hungry birds and other animals

venom

poison that some animals make; cobras, vipers, komodo dragons, Mexican beaded lizards and Gila monsters kill their prey with venom

rattle

venomous rattlesnakes have hollow scales at the ends of their tails; they shake them to make a warning sound

play dead

some reptiles, such as hognose snakes and chameleons, roll over and play dead if threatened; some predators won't eat animals they think are dead

drop tail

some lizards drop or lose their tails to escape enemies; new tails slowly grow

camouflage

colouring that makes animals look like their surroundings; many snakes and lizards that live in trees are green to help them blend in

mimicry

milk snake

coral snake

act of looking like something or someone else; the milksnake has brightly coloured skin that looks like the deadly coral snake; predators ignore the milksnake and look for something safer to eat

puffy throat

frilled lizards fan out the skin around their throats to scare off other animals

Reptile record holders

Large reptiles are easy to spot. Others are so small, you might miss them! Take a peek at these reptile record holders.

green anaconda

one of the world's longest snakes, the green anaconda, can grow more than 9 metres (30 feet) long; its size helps it kill large animals such as deer

dwarf gecko

at just 1.5 centimetres (0.6 inches) long, the dwarf gecko is the world's smallest lizard and reptile; it hides under leaves on rainforest floors

saltwater crocodile

the largest living reptile hides its 1,000-kilogram (2,220-pound) body below the water's surface; it bursts out of the water to grab large prey like kangaroos

Barbados thread snake

not all snakes are big;
the world's shortest snake
is only about 10 centimetres
(4 inches) long

leatherback turtle

the largest turtle grows to
1.8 metres (6 feet) long; it
weighs about 900 kilograms
(2,000 pounds), which is as
heavy as a small car

komodo dragon

the komodo dragon is the world's
largest lizard; it weighs about 130
kilograms (300 pounds) and grows
up to 3 metres (10 feet) long

speckled padloper

the smallest turtle grows up to
10 centimetres (4 inches) long;
its rocklike shell blends in with its
rocky habitat

Ancient reptiles

Dinosaurs were relatives of reptiles and lived on every continent. They died out about 65 million years ago. Today's alligators and crocodiles are related to dinosaurs, but birds are the closest living relatives of dinosaurs!

extinct

dinosaurs are extinct and no longer living anywhere in the world

fossil

remains or traces of living things preserved as rock; 200–million–year–old tuatara fossils closely match the skeletons of today's tuataras

archosaur

group of reptiles that came before dinosaurs and died out a long time ago; both dinosaurs and crocodiles are related to archosaurs; crocodiles first appeared about 220 million years ago

tyrannosaurus rex

tyrannosaurus rex was a huge, flesh-eating dinosaur; its closest living relative is the chicken

stegosaurus

dinosaur that fed on plants and had bony plates along its back, a small head and a long tail with spikes

triceratops

large dinosaur that ate plants and had three horns and a bony collar in the shape of a fan at the back of its head

Read more

Amazing Snakes (Exploring Nature), Barbara Taylor (Armadillo Books, 2013)

I Love My Pet Iguana, Aaron Carr (AV2 Weigl, 2013)

Reptiles (Animal Classification), Angela Royston (Raintree, 2016)

Websites

www.animals.nationalgeographic.com/animals/reptiles/
Learn about Nile crocodiles, Komodo dragons and more on this National Geographic website.

www.bbc.co.uk/nature/21458115
Read about the world's reptiles that are at risk of extinction.